The Little Book of Bob

Also by James Bowen

A Street Cat Named Bob

The World According to Bob

Bob: No Ordinary Cat

For the Love of Bob

Where in the World is Bob?

My Name is Bob

A Gift for Bob

The Little Book of Bob

James Bowen

THOMAS DUNNE BOOKS

NEW YORK

First published in the United States by Thomas Dunne Books, an imprint of St. Martin's Publishing Group

www.thomasdunnebooks.com

The Library of Congress Cataloging-in-Publication Data is available upon request.

ISBN 978-1-250-21536-9 (hardcover)
ISBN 978-1-250-21537-6 (ebook)

Our books may be purchased in bulk for promotional, educational, or business use. Please contact your local bookseller or the Macmillan Corporate and Premium Sales Department at 800-221-7945, extension 5442, or by email at MacmillanSpecialMarkets@macmillan.com.

Originally published in Great Britain by Hodder & Stoughton, an Hachette UK company

First U.S. Edition: October 2019

10 9 8 7 6 5 4 3 2 1

To Ron Richardson, always there for me,
no matter what.

Very little is needed to make a happy life; it is all within yourself, in your way of thinking.

Marcus Aurelius

I have studied many philosophers and many cats. The wisdom of cats is infinitely superior.

Hippolyte Taine

Contents

Introduction

Like most people, I've made bad choices in my life. More than a few of them.

My decision to adopt a ginger street cat named Bob definitely wasn't one, however. Quite the opposite; I'd say it was the wisest move I've ever made. In many ways, we saved each other. He had been injured when I found him in the spring of 2007 and I'd nursed him back to health.

He certainly rescued me. When I look back on it, my life had been a real mess before I met him. For a decade or more, I'd been an addict and had spent an extended period homeless, sleeping rough or in shelters. I had been down to my last chance – on my ninth life, if you like. I credit him with helping me to turn things around.

I've often thought about the life Bob led before we met. To judge by the wounds on his body when I met him, he'd been living a precarious existence. He had obviously got himself into a few scrapes. But how had he lived from day to day? Had he always been a street cat? Or had someone else looked after him before me? I had no idea.

Throughout our time together he has remained a puzzle. An enigma.

One thing I have known from the very beginning, however, is that he possesses a wisdom that is unusual, even in cats.

I don't know if this has anything to do with lessons he learned during that earlier, mysterious life, but it's as if he is some ancient philosopher who understands everything and everyone around him. As if he's seen it all before. Knows life inside out.

Nothing seems to faze him. He takes everything in his stride.

In the decade since we met, he's grown even wiser, in my eyes. My life has changed quite dramatically during that time, thanks to a series of memoirs about our life together and then a movie, *A Street Cat Named Bob*. He has adapted to the changes that have occurred in our fortunes with ease. He is as comfortable meeting people at book signings or film premieres as he was sitting on the pavement while I strummed my guitar in Covent Garden or sold *The Big Issue* outside the tube station at the Angel in north London.

I know it might sound strange or even slightly silly to say this about a cat, but I find him inspirational. Sometimes, simply sitting down and watching him is enough to set my mind whirring away. I'm fascinated by the way he conducts himself, the way he interacts with the world and responds to different situations. Even the way he lives his day-to-day routine. Being with him has opened my eyes to so much. Provoked so many thoughts. For the past ten years or more, he has genuinely been a kind of guru to me.

This book is a collection of some of the experiences and insights I've gained during my years with Bob. A guide to his street wisdom, if you like. I hope it helps you as much as he has helped me.

James Bowen
London, 2018

PART ONE

In Bob We Trust –
Lessons in Friendship

People often say that humans don't adopt cats; it's more a case of them adopting us. I suspect that is probably true. They are highly intelligent animals, after all. And deep down, I have a hunch they are smart enough to understand something that we humans too often overlook – the all-important value of friendship. I've certainly grown to appreciate it more – thanks to Bob.

Friendship Is a Pair of New Boots

Bob was a pretty rough-and-ready character when he came to live with me.

He didn't take kindly to being told off and could be a real handful if I stopped him from doing something. Before I had him neutered, he would lash out and scratch me. My hands bore the scars of his occasional tantrums.

I'd be lying if I said his behaviour didn't annoy me at times. But I had formed an instant affection for him and wanted our relationship to work.

At that time, I remember, I'd just bought myself a pair of black, army-style boots, from a local charity store. My old pair had literally fallen apart. The new pair did not quite fit me properly; the boots were a bit tight and had started to chafe and blister my feet. The best part of the day was taking them off.

It was as I slipped off the boots and let my feet breathe one evening, that it struck me.

Bob was pacing the flat, looking a little agitated. Earlier that evening, he had hissed at me when I'd tried to encourage him to use the litter tray I had brought into the house.

He was bound to feel uneasy with me and his new home, I thought to myself. Things I did were bound to rub him up the wrong way. But with patience, we would mould our friendship to fit each other's personality. We would get used to each other and our very different ways.

Our friendship was actually no different

to my new pair of boots. It was going to take time. There would be some discomfort. We'd irritate each other. But in the end, we'd fit each other just fine. And so it proved.

Free Spirits

The moment I knew Bob and I were destined to be together came, one unforgettable day, when he jumped on the bus to travel with me into London.

I had been flabbergasted. I'd shooed him away after he'd followed me to the bus stop from my flat and, as the bus had pulled away, had assumed he'd been left behind on the pavement. But suddenly, there he was, sitting on the seat next to me, curled up next to my guitar case as if he too was part of my luggage.

The bus conductor had smiled at me and asked me whether he was mine.

'I guess he must be,' I'd replied at the time, but I'd quickly come to realise that wasn't quite the case.

Bob is a force of nature, a free spirit. He wasn't mine. He wasn't a possession. I didn't own him then, nor do I own him now. We've chosen to be together in the present. But who knows whether we will be in the future? He will always be my friend, but he's free to leave whenever he wants.

I think that freedom is a key to any true friendship.

We Are All Stronger Together

I was cooking dinner one night, a few weeks after Bob and I got together. I was making spaghetti bolognese. Bob was curled up in the corner, watching me.

I'd put some music on the radio, boiled some water and was unwrapping the pack of dried spaghetti when the thought came to me. It was a distant memory from childhood, of a fable or fairytale about an old man teaching his children a valuable lesson using a bundle of sticks.

'See this, Bob,' I said, snapping a single strand of spaghetti, before dropping it into the pan of boiling water on the hob.

'That's you and me before we were friends. When we were on our own.'

I then picked up a thick bunch of spaghetti, bending it one way then the other, but failing to break it in half.

'And that's you and me now.'

He tilted his head at me as if I was slightly mad. I wasn't, of course. I'd never said a wiser word.

Bob could have been spending that night out on the streets. Cold, lonely and hungry. Similarly, I could still have been living hand-to-mouth as a homeless addict. Without any focus or goal in my life. But the fact was, we weren't. We'd found each other. And we were better, safer and healthier for it.

We are all stronger together than we are apart.

The Truest of Friends

People are always fascinated by the special bond that exists between Bob and me. How did we come to form such strong ties? I've come to understand that the answer is quite simple.

We live in a world where it's hard to have faith in very much at all. Politicians, institutions, people – they all seem to let us down at one time or another. I certainly felt that way. A lot of my troubles were self-inflicted, but they were also rooted in broken relationships and the feeling that I'd been unloved.

Our relationships with our pets offer an alternative. We can rely on them. They don't lie to us. They don't cheat on us. They don't let us down. Their affection for us – call it love, if you like – is unconditional.

Knowing that friendship is always there for you is not only an immense comfort. It is a source of strength, too.

A Friend in Need

Everyone has fair-weather friends. They are present when the times are good. Always around to share in the celebrations, the parties, the easy stuff. But when – as inevitably happens – life enters choppier waters, these people melt into the background, or worse, disappear altogether. That's not a true friend. A true friend is there for you in times of need. When there's nothing to be gained. Or worse. Something to be lost.

There were times when Bob was totally independent, happy to be left to his own devices. He would sleep where he wanted, when he wanted. He explored my flat and the wider world as he pleased.

But he also had an ability to know when he was needed. I spotted it first when I picked up a bad cold, a few weeks after we'd got together. I'd been lying in bed, coughing and spluttering away, feeling pretty sorry for myself. I'd noticed him curled up close to me, just a few feet away from my face. He was purring away rhythmically. It immediately comforted me.

Apart from anything else, it made me feel like I wasn't alone. The purring was rather soothing, too. But there was something else, a sense of companionship, a feeling that was unusual for me – of my life being shared with someone else.

He has retained this habit. He's always attentive when I feel low. Instinctively, he seems to know when it is time for him to be a friend.

I've come to see that friendship is like this. It is not about being there every moment of the day – it's about being there when it matters.

The Same Path

It is much more difficult for someone to understand the journey you have undertaken if they haven't walked down the same

path as you. That's why the strongest friend-
ships are often forged in the same fire. The
tougher the times you've been through, the
tighter the ties that bind you.

That's certainly the case with Bob and
me.

We've been through so much together.
Bad times and good times. We have travelled
so far down that same road that our paths
rarely diverge. It's probably why, since meeting, we have never gone our separate ways.

True Friends Just Understand

We all have bad days. We all experience
times when, for whatever reason, everything seems out of sorts. The world seems
off-kilter.

Often you can't explain it. Nor do you
want to. You simply want to close the door

and forget about everyone and everything. Call it what you want: depression, the blues, a bad-hair day. It all amounts to the same thing.

At times like this, I've noticed that Bob's friendship is subtly different. Sometimes, I won't even be aware he is present. He will tuck himself under the chair or the bed, near me. On stand-by.

It's as if he's sensitive to my mood; as if he knows I need space, but that I also need watching. He seems to understand.

Again, I've come to see that's the mark of a true friend. They grasp instinctively that sometimes you don't want endless questions about what has upset you. You don't want to have to explain yourself. You just want someone to understand your mood – and nothing else.

Sometimes You Need to Lose Something to Appreciate It

A few years ago, I had to spend a period in hospital after developing DVT, deep vein thrombosis, a painful condition in my leg. I was still young, not even thirty at that point, but lying restlessly in bed for hours on end was a real wake-up call. It made me realise I'd taken my health for granted. I'd assumed that I was invincible, that I would always be fit and well, despite the obvious damage I'd done to myself as an addict living on the streets.

To my surprise, the absence of Bob hit me almost as hard. He had become my ever-present companion by that point. Always there to cheer me up.

As a result, I missed him really badly when I was in hospital. For obvious reasons, he couldn't come along and visit me.

When I was discharged, that first night back in my flat with him was as big a boost to my spirits as any doctor's diagnosis or any medicine they could have dispensed for me in the hospital. Any spell away from him now reminds me of that time, and reinforces my appreciation of how lucky I am to have him in my life.

Sometimes – as with your health – you have to lose someone's friendship in order to appreciate its true value.

Friends Can Be a Good Influence

Bob and I were on the London underground, heading home one evening. There must have been a football match going on, because the tube carriage was crowded with rowdy fans wearing scarves and shirts. We were squeezed next to a group of them

– four young lads – who were in pretty lively mood.

We had just pulled off from a station when one of them started chanting his team's name really loudly, within inches of me. His shouts caught Bob completely by surprise, but he dealt with it as most hard-bitten London commuters would. He arched his back briefly then turned away from them, nuzzling his head into my coat, as if switching off from the hubbub around him.

I hadn't had the greatest day and wasn't impressed by the lad's behaviour,

'Can you not do that. It's scaring my cat,' I said, as politely as I could.

The four lads looked bemused. They exchanged glances and then laughed. They probably couldn't believe they'd been ticked off by a man with a cat on his shoulder. But to be fair, they nodded at me as if in acknowledgment. They remained reasonably well-behaved until they got off the train, leaving me and Bob to ourselves.

A few years earlier, I would definitely have been more vocal. I might even have lost my temper. But tonight, I'd taken the view they were just young lads. They weren't doing any harm. I had bitten my tongue and let it go. I'd cut them some slack. I had a feeling I had Bob to thank for that.

He had helped me to see the world differently. Given me someone else to care for, someone else to think about. A responsibility that I hadn't really experienced before. And, perhaps without me even thinking about it, he had made me less self-centred. Kinder, more thoughtful, too.

Friends Are Free to Make Fools of Themselves

Every now and again, Bob will do something totally unpredictable. He might – for no apparent reason – decide to drape himself across the back of the sofa, stretching himself out in the most physically impossible position imaginable, seeming to defy the laws of gravity as he sleeps. Equally, he might suddenly start jumping and chasing around the room as if in pursuit of a fly or a wasp. His target is completely invisible – to me, at least.

If it were someone I didn't know well, I might worry. I might fret about the fact that he was acting out of character. That he's not the cat I once thought he was. But I don't. Because it's Bob, my best friend – I don't bat an eyelid.

I don't sit there analysing what has got into him, wondering whether there's some deep psychological issue. I watch and laugh. (Unless he's really doing damage to the furniture, of course.)

One of the great blessings of a strong friendship is that it gives you the freedom to be yourselves together, to let your hair down and go a little bit crazy every now and again. You know each other well enough not to take it seriously. It doesn't change anything long-term.

Share Your Good Fortune

To say that Bob transformed my fortunes is something of an understatement. In the ten years we've been together, my life has changed beyond all recognition. When we first teamed up, we had busked and sold *The Big Issue* together, living pretty much hand-to-mouth. In the past few years our job has been very different: appearing at public events and signings and on television to promote the books and the movie.

I'd like to think I haven't changed too much in that time. It's probably for others to judge that ultimately. But I can say with absolute certainty that Bob hasn't altered one tiny bit. He has remained the same, Zen-like cat through-out. He has travelled the world, met thousands of people, appeared on count-less TV shows. Yet he has remained chilled and content, from Berlin to Tokyo, Truro to Glasgow.

He has had his odd moment of grumpi-ness. Who doesn't? But in the main, he has barely uttered a growl of complaint. He simply sits there swishing his tail rhythmic-ally, sometimes purring quietly, putting a smile on people's faces as he does so, includ-ing mine. The joy it gives me to see him bringing such happiness to others is beyond words. The knowledge that he is happy and content in doing so makes it even more precious.

They say that a problem shared is a prob-lem halved. Well, I think the opposite is also true. Good fortune shared is good fortune doubled.

Faith in Friends Repays Itself

My stomach was churning as I led Bob in front of the lights and cameras that had been set up on an alleyway between Bow Street and Drury Lane.

It was a couple of weeks into the filming of *A Street Cat Named Bob* and the director Roger Spottiswoode was keen to experiment with Bob 'acting' in a scene. I had been unsure, but he and the producer Adam Rolston had persuaded me that this was a good opportunity.

The scene they had chosen involved Luke Treadaway, the actor playing me, sitting on the pavement, busking. It was a scene Bob knew inside out – he'd lived it for years.

But as I led him there I was racked with doubt. Would he be happy doing this?

Even if he was, would he be able to do what was required of him? I didn't want to let anyone down. And I certainly didn't want to waste the very expensive film crew's time.

The cameras had barely begun rolling when Bob did something amazing. As the stream of extras walked past, dropping and clinking coins into the guitar case, Bob began nodding at each of them, as if to say 'thanks'.

The crew's faces were a picture. You could see people asking themselves the same question: 'Did I just see what I just saw?' They had. And they saw it again on the next 'take', and the next one.

From then on, Bob appeared in as many scenes as was possible. He was working alongside a team of specialist ginger cats that had been brought over from Canada and trained to do the more difficult, action shots. Bob couldn't do those. They were left to his 'bobbelgangers'.

I learned a huge amount during those few, surreal weeks. But the lesson Bob taught me that night was perhaps one of the most important. Have faith. Believe in the friends who believe in you. If you do, they will repay that faith.

You Can't Lose a Real Friend

During the course of our years together, Bob has run away from me twice. Both incidents happened early on during our time together when Bob got scared, first by a street entertainer and then by a very aggressive dog.

We were reunited on each occasion, but it didn't mean the separations weren't hard. During the – thankfully brief – periods that

Bob and I were apart, I felt a nagging pain, as if there was something wrong with a part of me. It was only afterwards that I recognised what that meant.

The only friends you can lose are those who aren't really friends at all.

You can never lose a true friend. Even if you are separated. That friendship lives on inside you. It is a part of each of you. It doesn't go away.

PART TWO

It's a Bob's Life – What We Need to Be Happy

We are all in search of fulfilment. But how and where do we find it? What are the foundation stones, the must-have ingredients for a contented existence? In other words, what do we need to be happy?

It's something I've often asked myself during my past decade with Bob. He has been instrumental in guiding me to some of the answers.

We All Need to Be Noticed

Once he and I had settled into our life together, Bob loved nothing more than being stroked or fussed over. I got the distinct impression that no one had spoiled him for a very long time, that he had been deprived of attention.

It pleased me that I was able to provide that attention, but it upset me, too. I kept imagining his previous life, kept seeing him sleeping in alleyways, being ignored by people. Getting no attention at all.

I didn't need to imagine what that felt like. I knew all too well from my time living on the streets. Like him I'd been ignored, marginalised; I'd disappeared, become an invisible man. And so I also understood that his happiness with me was a reaction to being made to feel important. Special.

We all need to be noticed. We all need to feel we are important. That we are needed.

We All Need a Routine

The routine into which we eventually settled was key in making Bob a calmer, more contented cat. He was less animated and agitated if he ate at the same time: first thing in the morning and early in the evening, around six. If he was then free to have a nap, he became even less erratic. Less on edge.

Later on too, as our relationship settled into a regular working pattern, that routine became even more entrenched. By then it was summertime and I would head into Covent Garden to busk later in the day.

The crowds were more numerous – and generous – in the late afternoon and evening.

It generally took us three quarters of an hour or so to get into the city, so in order to make the evening rush, we'd need to leave home before 5 p.m. Bob used to head to the door at 4.30 p.m. exactly. He'd finish off whatever food he had, then position himself there. It was as if he was saying: 'Hurry up, mate, we've got a bus to catch.'

I could have set my watch to him. In fact, on more than one occasion he had acted as an alarm, hurrying me up when my mind was elsewhere.

I now see that need for certainty is something universal – something that each and every one of us feels. Routine gives us parameters, but more importantly, it makes us feel secure.

We All Need Our Space

The more I got to know Bob – and his feline ways – the more I got to see that he and I were not so different after all. And once I realised that, I also began to understand what would make him feel at home.

For example, I had heard that territory is hugely important to cats. It's why they use the scent glands on their paws and in their claws to leave scent trails wherever they go. It is why they rub up and scratch furniture – and us, apparently. It provides them with assurance that their space is 'safe'.

Early on I had dissuaded Bob from doing it, gently pushing him away when he started scratching at the legs of a battered old chair in the corner.

It was when a friend visited me with his dog, a black Labrador, that the penny dropped. On first seeing the dog, Bob arched his back, made hissing noises and retreated to a safe corner. The dog barked back a couple of times, but soon settled. Bob watched him like a hawk. The minute the dog was out of the door, he leapt into action, striding around the flat, rubbing and scratching at everything.

'He's reclaiming his territory,' I said to myself.

We all like our space. We all prefer it to be a certain way and 'mark' it so that it is identifiably ours with our choice of furniture, colour schemes, paintings and photos on the wall. And we can get upset if other people invade that space and disrupt the balance.

Ever since then, I have let Bob get on with it. He rubs up against me, the furniture, door frames, radiators. Anything that makes him feel like his territory is established – and safe.

We All Need to Be Independent

Bob has always been self-sufficient. I think it stems from his days on the streets, looking after himself.

He seems to have learned that, if you need something in life, it is usually best to rely on yourself to provide it. The chances are that no one else will.

Early on, for instance, he learned to open cupboard doors so that he could look for food. He also learned to go to the toilet on his own, and once – to my amazement – used the toilet in my flat.

In recent years, he has got even more resourceful. In my new house, Bob can turn the handles on doors, especially the one leading into the kitchen, where I keep his food and water bowl on the floor.

Even more impressively, he has learned how to turn the tap on one of the sinks upstairs. He loves watching the running water and, when he's feeling a bit over-heated, will dip his paw in and lick it to quench his thirst.

It always makes me smile. But it also reinforces something important. We all need to be independent. We all need to feel like we can control our lives.

We All Want to Feel Protected

We were out in central London one day, early on in our time together, when there was a loud explosion nearby. At first there was panic. We live in dangerous times. People didn't know what had happened, whether to hide or run for safety. After a while, however, it calmed down.

Bob had been walking alongside me. He had reacted to the bang instantly and had jumped up on to my shoulders. I'd been too wrapped up in the drama to really notice. But as things calmed down, I realised that he was still there – wrapped tightly around my neck.

He'd taken to riding on my shoulders when we were walking around central London, but this was the first time I'd seen him jump there as a reflex, as if seeking out

42

a safe haven. I was touched. It underlined the feeling I had that he felt safe, protected in my company. And that safety was one of the reasons why he had decided to live with me.

We all need to feel that safety. That we are protected by someone or something.

We All Need to Be Ourselves

I had taken Bob into the park off the Embankment, near where we had been busking around Charing Cross station. I decided to sit down and take a break, while he did his business in the bushes.

He was attached to a long, string lead, which I could lengthen. After a while I felt a tugging on the line, as if I was a fisherman who had landed a fish. He was trying to get deeper into the bush. I stood up and fed him some more string. I assumed he wanted to find the right spot.

It was a couple of minutes later when he emerged. He did so with a small mouse in his teeth. It was alive and wriggling, desperately trying to escape. I was about to intervene, when the mouse managed to escape. Bob had placed it on the ground for a second and it had made a run for it. It scampered off at lightning speed.

I shouldn't have been surprised. Cats are predatory creatures. If we were going to be out in the world together, incidents like this were going to happen. It brought something home to me.

None of us are angels. We are all imperfect creatures. But we are who we are. It is in our nature. So many people try to change others – to mould them into something they are not. I wasn't going to do that.

Bob is a strong personality and I wanted him to be himself. Looking back on it, I think it was another of the reasons he stayed with me. None of us want to be prisoners of other people's ideas about who we should be. We all need to be free to be ourselves.

We All Need Something to Believe In

We were sitting on the pavement in the West End one evening, when a well-dressed guy emerged from the tube station concourse, walked to a spot a dozen or so metres from us and erected a placard.

It read: 'Believe in the Lord'.

I left him to it. My salvation depended on selling another dozen copies of *The Big Issue* before the evening rush hour ended.

The guy soon started preaching, reading from the Bible, but few people paid him any attention. Some were openly abusive to him.

I admired his resilience. He believed in something, I thought to myself.

For a moment I watched him, fascinated, a question forming in my mind.

Hmm, I thought. What do I believe in?

Just then Bob perked up and let out a meow. It was his 'I'm hungry' meow.

I reached into my rucksack and dug out a treat, then bent down to feed him. He leaned into my hand and rubbed his head against it, purring quietly.

I smiled to myself. I had my answer.

'You are what I believe in, Bob,' I said.

It was true. He had given me a new approach to life. A different perspective. He'd also given me purpose. Something to focus on, a shape to my day-to-day life. A structure that hadn't been there before.

In some sense, Bob must have felt the same way, too. He needed something to believe in as well, I guess. I think we all do.

We All Need Our Own Patch

It was a sunny weekend afternoon, a short time after Bob and I had moved into our new house, in the Surrey suburbs. I'd come downstairs to find Bob wasn't anywhere to be seen.

Instinctively I went out into the small garden where, in the past few days, he had begun to explore his new surroundings, sniffing the grass and the plants and watching the birds in the trees overhead. Sure enough, I glimpsed his distinctive ginger coat disappearing over the garden fence, backing on to some open ground beyond.

I was surprised. Bob wasn't a cat that wandered particularly. He liked to stay close to home. So whilst I was concerned, I didn't panic immediately.

After a couple of hours, however, I began to grow more nervous. Evening was closing in and I didn't want him to be out overnight. So I returned to the garden and started shouting for him. There was no sign of him.

I was just about to head back into the house when I heard noises. I recognised the sound instantly: it was two cats confronting each other.

I found Bob and a large, black cat a few feet apart on the fence alongside the house. The instant he saw me, Bob leapt off and literally jumped into my arms. It was as if we'd been separated for years – not a few hours.

It was obvious what had been going on. He had been doing what everyone needs to do to a greater or lesser extent when they move home, getting to know the lie of the land, marking out his own patch. Satisfied that he'd done that, he had run for home. He hasn't strayed from the garden since.

We All Need Things to Treasure

The sound of me doing the weekly hoovering in the living room had sent Bob scuttling off upstairs. He didn't much like it.

I'd not cleaned under the sofa for a while, so decided to slide it across the carpet to get the hoover underneath. I had been amazed at what I found.

It was like an Aladdin's cave of Bob's stuff.

He is regularly given and sent toys by fans from all over the world and plays with lots of them. Somehow, he had dragged a collection of toy animals, balls and assorted toys here. But this wasn't all. Bob had developed a habit of playing with plastic bottle lids that he found in the kitchen.

He had somehow hoarded about a dozen of them as well.

I threw the lids in the bin, but put the toys back into the large box in the hall.

I was intrigued. Why had he hoarded like this?

It wasn't too long after we had moved house. Had he been concerned that this new environment may contain other cats or animals who might steal his toys? Or was it his way of making sure his toys were safe from me? He had seen me bring in new furniture – and get rid of some other things. Was he concerned about me throwing his toys away?

Whatever the explanation, one thing was clear. These things were important to him. Knowing they were there made him feel safe and secure. Thinking about it, again, I realised that I was no different.

I was protective of certain things – photos, gifts from fans, books, mementoes from my travels – and had made sure I had safe places to keep them, in my living room and office. It was less to do with the fact they were worth anything, but more because they were of immense value to me.

It's all part of that need to feel that our home – and the precious things that make it feel like a home – are safe and secure.

We All Need Insecurity, Too

I had just moved into my new home and taken delivery of some flatpack furniture, which I'd slowly begun assembling. The hallway was filled with empty cardboard boxes, plastic bubble wrap and bits of polystyrene.

Bob, naturally, was fascinated by this. To him the chaotic pile of rubbish was an adventure playground, which he had to explore at every possible opportunity.

I had just finished putting together a coffee table in the living room when I noticed him playing there.

He was fixated by the bubble wrap and polystyrene. He was fascinated by the squeaking noises they made. He was also drawn to the boxes. One at a time, he climbed into the smaller ones, as if testing them to see which would make the best bed later. I didn't have the heart to tell him that it was all going into a recycling bin when I finished assembling everything.

The taller cardboard boxes that had contained the cabinets, were leaning up against each other, supporting each other like some sort of abstract art sculpture. Bob decided to climb it. The construction was very flimsy and I had a feeling he would be too heavy, but left him to it.

Sure enough, he'd just scaled the peak of the little cardboard mountain when *whoomph*, the whole edifice collapsed. Nimble and agile creature that he was, he jumped off, looking slightly miffed that his fun had been cut short.

I couldn't stop myself from laughing.

It struck me that we all need security, but sometimes we need insecurity, too. Some surprise elements that provide us with challenges and chances to learn. It helps us to grow. To learn. And if we can do so while having some fun as well, then all the better.

PART THREE

Being Bob – How to Get the Most Out of Life

Cats are experts at getting the most from life. They know what they want and know how to get it. And they execute their plans with laser-like efficiency. Bob is a master at squeezing the most from every day. He has strategies for success that would put even the most brilliant business minds to shame.

But he also seems to know how to enjoy and savour life, too. How to extract the positive from every situation. How to have the maximum fun. Spending time with him has opened my eyes to some of the secrets of his success. And it's made me wonder whether – at least, every now and again – we'd all benefit from being a little like Bob.

Think Slow, Act Fast

It is fascinating to watch the way Bob makes a decision. Before he does so, he will often sit there, like some little Buddha, slowly mulling over the choices in front of him. You can almost hear the machinations in his brain. Tick. Tick. Tick.

It doesn't matter what it is. He might be wondering whether to go for a stretch, a snooze or head to his bowl for something to eat. He will only take action when he's ready. Not a second earlier, not a second later.

When he makes his move, however, he is decisive. *Boom*. There's no hesitation. He knows what he wants and how to get it. And he generally does. He acts fast and gets results.

In a world where too many of us are indecisive or make snap decisions that we come to regret, we'd do well to take a leaf out of Bob's book.

To think slow, but act fast.

Believe in Yourself

Cats aren't weighed down by a lack of self-confidence. They don't harbour any self-doubt, at all. As far as we can tell, at least.

They seem to know what they want and are determined to get it.

I have a strong feeling that this is one of the keys to Bob's general wellbeing. He always exudes self-confidence. He seems totally comfortable in his own skin. We could all learn from it. We are all weighed down by insecurities and self-doubt.

I know it isn't easy, but we all have strengths and qualities that we can draw upon to give us confidence in ourselves. If we believe in ourselves, the world looks a very different place.

Our Happiness Lies Within

Bob can spend hours entertaining himself. He can fill half the day lying on the window-sill, watching the world go by. At our old flat in north London, he would watch the clouds floating by, the rain falling, the people and traffic passing by – anything and everything had the potential to entertain him. He's the same at our new home. He will lie there staring out into the garden, quietly mesmerised by the world outside.

Watching him, it often strikes me that he embodies something very simple, yet very profound. Something that a lot of people struggle to understand. There's a very famous Chinese saying: 'Happiness is the absence of the striving for happiness.'

What I think that means is that our happiness isn't dependent on others. It isn't something that we have to chase after. It actually lies within ourselves.

Bob seems to know that.

Open Your Eyes

During his days on the street, Bob loved nothing more than sitting with me on the pavement on a sunny day, quietly watching the world rushing past. He would take in everything. In his own laid-back way, of course.

Sometimes it would seem like his eyes were closed, but he missed nothing. It might be a bird scavenging for food in a nearby bin, a street performer setting up, a passer-by with an interesting outfit. He would quietly raise his head and zoom in. He would then watch or listen; fascinated, absorbing it all. It was as if he knew there was something to be gained from the experience. Something new, enlightening or simply entertaining to see.

We walk around with our eyes open, but there are times when we might as well have them closed. We are too busy, too wrapped up in our day-to-day lives to see what's in front of us.

We miss out on so much as a result.

There's Wonder All Around Us

Bob has an amazing effect on people. Men and women would often come across him lying on the pavement and be moved to tears. It was as if they'd discovered hidden treasure or a long lost relative. They would sit down and stroke him for a few minutes and be transformed. And often they weren't even cat lovers.

It made me wonder about the way we see the world. When people are looking for inspiration, they always tend to look upwards. To the skies. To the heavens. It's only natural. We are always being told that it's where the real wonder of life lies. Reach for the stars, we are told. Never reach for the gutter.

And yet, it seemed to me, at least, that by looking for inspiration in unexpected places, our imaginations, our minds – and best of all our hearts – might be opened up even more.

There is beauty and wonder there, too, if we only take the trouble to see it.

If You See a Chance, Take It

Like every other cat in the world, Bob is an opportunist. He will make the most of any opportunity that is presented to him.

It might be the offer of a snack or a treat. It might be an invitation to have his tummy tickled or go off for an exploratory walk in the bushes in the park. Whatever it is, his attitude is – if it's there, I am going to accept it.

In those situations, he doesn't humm and haah endlessly. He doesn't weigh up the pros and cons for very long. He sees the door – and then goes through it. There are times in all our lives, when we would do well to take the same approach.

If you see a chance, take it.

Don't Dwell on the Small Stuff

There's a well known book called 'Don't Sweat the Small Stuff'. Its basic message is simple: don't fixate on the tiny irritations or setbacks in life. Let them go. Put them into the proper perspective. Don't turn them into big stuff that makes you stressed and unhappy.

Bob seems to instinctively operate according to that philosophy.

It's rare that he gets into a confrontation with another cat or a dog, for instance, but even if he does, he doesn't seem to let it get under his skin. Once that confrontation has run its course, he will almost always walk away. Regardless of the outcome.

We humans don't do this easily. We are prone to seek revenge or retribution. To stew on even the smallest things, take them personally. I can't know exactly what goes on in Bob's brain, but he seems to simply gets on with it. It's as if he knows that feeling angry or vengeful is a waste of time. I have a strong suspicion that it's one of the reasons he lives such a seemingly contented existence.

Be Appreciative

Like all cats, Bob seems to live in the present. Who knows whether he thinks about the past, or the future? What's quite clear is that in his day-to-day life, he deals in the here and now.

If he wants to grab a snooze, it doesn't matter if it is on a cold pavement or on a comfortable sofa. It makes no difference to him. He will curl himself up and nod off, oblivious to whatever is going on around him.

It's the same at meal times. It doesn't matter if his food bowl contains a few handfuls of biscuit or a feast of gourmet tuna, he will gobble it down just the same. His attitude is: that's my meal. I'll eat what's in front of me.

I've often watched him and wondered whether there's a lesson there for all of us. The fact is that none of us is ever going to get everything that we want in life. None of us. We can work and strive to make things better, but we will never get all we want. It's impossible.

And that means that, as we go through life, we have a choice.

We can either get wrapped up in that: be obsessed with what we don't have, and the fact that we won't ever have it. Or we can appreciate what we do have.

Seize Each Day

I watch Bob some mornings and envy him. He wakes himself up, tucks into his breakfast and heads into his new day unencumbered by what happened yesterday or the day before.

To him, each morning marks the beginning of not only a new day, but a new opportunity to be content and happy. A chance to enjoy all that life has to offer him.

I often tell myself that it's not a bad philosophy to adopt. Especially when life seems hard. If you can forget about what happened yesterday and treat today as a fresh start, you are already halfway towards ensuring that today is a better one.

Know Your Limitations

For all his confidence, it is rare that Bob bites off more than he can chew. It's as if he knows his limitations. He is aware not to be too ambitious.

It's almost as though he knows that old Chinese saying: 'A bird can roost but on one branch and a mouse can drink no more than its fill from a river.'

It is something I tell myself often.

We should all know – and accept – our limitations.

There's Something Good in Every Day

Life on the streets could be miserable. I was ignored, abused – even spat at, on occasion.

But Bob was always there to cheer me up. It might be a silly thing he did, or simply a moment with him on the bus when he curled up next to me. Whenever he did that, I was reminded of something universal.

While, every day may not be good, there's something good in every day.

Let the Sun Shine In

Bob and I spent much of our first summer together sitting on the pavement near Covent Garden, busking in the rush hour. It wasn't the greatest of summers, weather-wise. The days were often overcast, the sun was an infrequent visitor.

Whenever it did appear in the skies, however, I noticed that it had an instant effect on Bob. He would spend most of his days curled up in a ball, quietly watching the flow of tourists and shoppers rushing past us.

The moment the sun arrived in the sky above us, though, he was a cat on a mission. He would begin shifting himself around, moving in and out of the shadows as he worked out the sunniest spot. He would then stretch his body out on the floor, elongating himself so as to get the maximum benefit.

Often it would be a fleeting opportunity. The sun would quickly disappear behind a new, passing cloud. But it didn't bother Bob one bit. He was always determined to make the absolute most of every ray of sunshine that was available.

It always made me smile to myself. I was full of admiration for him – and his philosophy. Life is short. Sometimes you have to squeeze every ounce of joy and pleasure you can from it. The sun doesn't always shine. If it's there, you should let it in.

Pick Your Battles

It was a bright summer's day and Bob was facing a dilemma. On the one hand, he was very happy lying on the sill of the open window as the sun streamed into our living room. On the other he was irritated by the bees that had been attracted to the flowers at the top of the garden near the window. He wanted them to buzz off.

For a few moments, I watched him weighing up his options. He was clearly asking himself: 'Can I get them?'

If it had been inside the house, it would have been a different story. But it was clear it would take a precision strike to leap through the window out on to the flower bed and to catch the bees. It was almost impossible, a million to one shot, but he kept mulling it over. Along with something else.

The other thing that was annoying him was a box of tissues on the sill. He'd parked himself tight up against it and was clearly unhappy that it was there. The sun was shining at its brightest in that exact spot.

It took him a minute or so to complete his calculations. As he did so, he looked back and forth between the bees outside and the box of tissue next to him. What to do?

When he made his move, it was decisive. In a smooth movement, he swished at the tissue box with his paw, flipping it off the sill on to the floor so that he now had the best spot. He then proceeded to splay himself out on the sill, soaking up the sunshine. The bees were forgotten.

It was an object lesson. If you are faced with a problem that you can do something about – then do something. But if you can't do anything – let it go.

Focus on what you can change. Forget about what you cannot. Life will be much simpler and enjoyable if you do.

Curiosity Doesn't Kill the Cat

If there's one expression that leaves me scratching my head, it is this: curiosity killed the cat.

I really don't get it. Curiosity, to my mind, is an intrinsic part of a cat's make-up. It is actually a life-saver, something that adds to their day-to-day existence.

Bob certainly loves exploring. Wherever we go, he will scout out his surroundings. He won't sit down contentedly until he's checked out the location fully. He will spend ages sniffing and shoving his head into nooks and crannies, rooting around until he is satisfied he has seen all there is to see.

It's partly an instinctive cat trait. He wants to feel safe and secure. He is marking out his territory. But it's partly, too, because he's curious – and, to judge from the way he wags his tail and nonchalantly strolls around, exploring the world around him makes him happy.

Too many of us lead incurious lives. Too many of us are afraid to try something new. Too many want to stick to the well-worn path, rather than following the uncharted one where we can leave our own trail. We should all embrace the unknown sometimes.

Curiosity doesn't kill anyone or anything. Quite the opposite – it is the source of some of the best things in life.

Always Enjoy the Journey

We were out walking in a nearby park one windy, autumn day, when Bob spotted a small pile of fallen leaves. They had been blown by the wind and had formed into a small pyramid. Bob jogged over to it, then waded into the pile until he was so deep into the leaves I could barely see his legs. He then began thrashing away, frantically clearing leaves away with his paws.

It was hilarious. For a while he was lost in a flurry of brown, gold and silver leaves.

It was impossible for me to know what was going through his mind. Perhaps he had decided there was something hidden under the leaves? Maybe he smelled a mouse or some food?

It wasn't long before the pyramid had been flattened, reduced to a blanket of leaves. Sure enough, there was something lying on the grass now, glinting in the afternoon sun. Unfortunately, it wasn't as exciting as Bob might have hoped. It was a battered, old Coke can.

He nudged it with his nose, to check it was as unpromising as it appeared. He then jogged away, eager to explore another, smaller pile of leaves, the disappointment of the previous one already forgotten.

Sitting on a bench nearby, watching the scene unfold, I couldn't help smiling. I was reminded me of that old saying: 'To travel hopefully is a better thing than to arrive'. We place so much emphasis on achieving our goals, on reaching our destinations, that we often forget to enjoy the journey.

We should follow Bob's example and simply relish the journey for what it is, regardless of where it takes us.

Take Things Little by Little

I was working in my living room one morning, when I heard a noise in the kitchen.

I found Bob standing at the foot of the fridge looking up, fixated on something.

One of his favourite treat sticks was balancing precariously on the edge of the fridge. I must have left it there.

It wasn't long before his teatime, and I didn't want him snacking now. So I ignored it and went back to work. I was writing a reply to an email that had made me a little angry. I wanted to vent my frustration.

Out of the corner of my eye, I saw him pacing around. He then jumped up on to the worktop near the fridge, about five feet away from the treat.

He had a dilemma. If he jumped up at it and nudged the fridge, he risked knocking the treat down the side where he would never be able to get to it. He was sitting there studying the situation. Weighing up his options.

I looked away, returning to my email.

A moment or two later, I looked again. Bob had now nudged a packet of biscuits into position beneath the treat and was standing on it, stretching upwards. With the most delicate movement of his paw, he nudged the treat in the right direction. He then got down, repositioned himself and did it again. He did that three times, but then on the fourth, the treat tipped off the edge and fell . . . on to the kitchen floor.

Mission accomplished.

I'd written a rather harsh email, but hadn't yet hit 'send'. As I fed Bob the contents of the treat, I decided against it. I did so later, but in more temperate language. And I got the result I wanted in the process.

Sometimes you have to achieve your goals by stealth. Intelligently. Patiently.

Little by little.

PART FOUR

Bob vs the World – How to Survive All That Life Throws at Us

It is often said that knowledge comes from learning, while wisdom comes from living. It has always struck me as being very true. So much of our so-called knowledge comes to us second-hand, from books, through film or television. Very few of us know things through first-hand experience.

I am frequently reminded of this when I look at Bob. He has not learned about life second-hand. All the wisdom he has acquired has come to him the hard way, from the years he spent on the streets, coping with people and situations of all kinds.

It is why I have always found it so interesting to try to understand that wisdom. And why it is so valuable. He has taught me a lot about coping with – and maybe even learning from – everything life has to throw at us.

Don't Let a Bad Yesterday
Spoil a Good Today

Bob's ability to shake off bad experiences was summed up by an experience we had one evening in central London. We had been heading home after a busy day doing interviews and promoting the movie, *A Street Cat Named Bob*.

I was about to hail a cab, when someone started shouting at me. It was a fairly well-to-do lady, probably in her sixties. She was in an animated state, waving a stick at me.

'That's cruelty to animals,' she shouted. 'You shouldn't have him on a lead. I'm going to report you to the RSPCA.'

I stopped and tried to talk to her. But she wasn't having any of it.

Bob had sensed that she wasn't a kind soul and had positioned himself defensively on my shoulder. I knew from experience that if this lady made a move, Bob would lash out at her. I really didn't want that to happen. That wasn't the kind of publicity we wanted! Fortunately, a black cab appeared with its yellow lights on. I hailed it and jumped in.

On the drive home, it ate away at me. I'd worked so hard all day. I'd spoken to journalists and TV presenters for hours, constantly promoting the positive, hopeful message of our story. The exchange with the lady in the street had lasted for less than a minute, but it had somehow spoiled the previous eight or nine hours.

But then I looked at Bob, lying on the leather seat of the cab, licking himself and gently purring away. He looked completely content. The confrontation with the woman had set him on edge as well. But he had brushed it off. It had been forgotten.

'You're right,' I said to him. 'What's the old expression: you shouldn't let a good today be ruined by a bad yesterday.'

Wisdom Is the Daughter of Experience

Since his earliest days with me, Bob has always seemed at his most focused when he feels under threat. His eyes dart around, his ears prick up and his tail points upwards. It's as if he is primed for anything – and prepared for the worst.

This is natural, animal instinct, of course, but I've often wondered whether it is also to do with his background, the hardships he suffered during his early days on the streets. Was he once attacked by a dog, for instance?

Is that why he is wary of some aggressive breeds?

Regardless of the past, the key thing is that he has learned from that experience. Wisdom, in his case, is very much the daughter of experience. The wisest of us are those that, like Bob, draw the biggest lessons from the hardship life throws at us.

Don't Be Ruled by Fear

Like all of us, Bob has a few dislikes and quirks. A few things that make him bristle or grow restless. He loathes the sound that lorries with hydraulic brakes make, for example. He can also get agitated by aggressive dogs and people. He doesn't like really loud music too much either, especially now he's getting older.

In general, however, he allows little to frighten or upset him. He relies on his experience. He simply keeps his eyes and ears – and his highly sensitive whiskers – open. And if he is unsure of something or someone, he reacts immediately. He will fight, freeze or take flight. He will deal with the situation decisively.

We seem to live in a world that is now filled with anxieties. People are crippled by fears, some genuine, but some completely irrational. We could all learn a lesson from Bob. He is careful and keeps his eyes open. But he doesn't let fear rule his world.

Don't Judge a Book by its Cover

Spending his days and nights on the streets, Bob saw human nature at its best and worst. Most of those he came across were kind to him, but some were mean. It gave him a very strong instinct about people.

Now if he senses a good, warm-hearted person, he calmly lets them approach and stroke him. But Bob can sniff or spot someone who is out to hurt or harm him from a mile away. And if he feels a threat, he soon lets them know. His hiss is quite something to behold. He has protected me from potential threats on more than one occasion.

What's important is that his judgment has nothing to do with appearances. How someone looks, the way they dress, or the colour of their skin. It's about what's going on inside, whether they are a good person or a bad one.

He never judges a book by its cover.

Guard Against Unguarded Thoughts

I always try to follow Bob's example. I do my best to judge people not by their appearance, but by the person I sense is inside.

It doesn't always work.

One morning during the filming of the movie in Covent Garden, I spotted a guy hovering a short distance away from where Bob and I were waiting to be called in front of the cameras.

He was a tall, lean figure in a scruffy denim jacket, jeans and trainers. He seemed on edge. I was wary immediately. There was a lot of expensive equipment around. Who knew what his intentions were? Was he planning on stealing something? Or worse, harming Bob?

I moved towards him.

'Whatever idea you might have, mate, forget it,' I said.

He looked confused.

'No, James. I'm not here to cause trouble. I'm Simon.'

Now it was my turn to be confused.

'Simon? Simon who? And how do you know my name?' He smiled.

'Simon from Centre Point. Five years ago. We shared a room. Don't you remember?'

I just froze.

'Oh my God.'

The two of us embraced like the long-lost friends we were.

Years earlier, we'd both been homeless and had taken refuge at the same charity centre. We'd drifted apart. Simon now lived in Glasgow, but had heard of Bob and me and come to see us. He'd been keeping a respectful distance, waiting for filming to end before coming to say hello.

It was a sobering reminder. When I was on the streets, people had always jumped to the wrong conclusions about me. Just because I was busking, it didn't mean I was a bad person. Now I'd been guilty of the same thing. I'd failed to abide by Bob's lesson and judged a book by its cover.

There's another old saying: 'Your worst enemy cannot harm you as much as your own unguarded thoughts.' This encounter taught me to be on guard more often.

Keep Facing the Sun

The abuse I received working on the streets was a constant part of my life. Almost every day someone would shout something behind my back. You never get used to it, but you do learn to live with it.

There were times when I would bite, and engage the person abusing me. It was a pointless exercise, however. There was no benefit in interacting with people, who – in all honesty – didn't deserve any interaction in the first place. I only upset myself by doing so.

Having Bob with me helped enormously. He almost physically forced me to take a different approach. He would sit on my shoulders, his face pointing forward, looking ahead rather than back. It struck me one sunny, summer's evening, while we were walking through Covent Garden, heading towards Leicester Square where I was due to meet a friend. Some idiot had just shouted abuse at me, but I ignored it. I pressed on with Bob on my shoulder, heading towards the sun, setting to the west.

'What's the old saying, Bob?' I said quietly to him. 'Keep your face always towards the sunshine – and the shadows will fall behind you.'

Sometimes Not Getting What You Want Is Good for You

There's an old Buddhist saying: 'Sometimes not getting what you want is a wonderful stroke of luck.' I hadn't really understood its full meaning until early on during my time with Bob, when my life took a dramatic turn.

Bob and I had been struggling to make ends meet busking around Covent Garden. I'd regularly run into trouble with the authorities and had a particularly bad relationship with the staff at the Covent Garden tube station, who objected to me and Bob sitting outside. Matters had come to a head when I'd been falsely accused of abusing a ticket inspector. I had been arrested and stuck in a prison cell overnight.

I'd been cleared of the charge eventually, but it had given me a wake-up call. I'd dreamed of using my busking as a launching pad for a musical career. But a night in a cold cell had made me realise – in the short term, at least – I simply wasn't going to be able to achieve that. I had Bob to care for, as well as myself. I had to make a change.

As it turned out, it was the best thing that could have happened to me. Instead I started selling *The Big Issue*, initially in the West End, but then at the Angel in Islington. It was there that my life was transformed. I was spotted by a literary agent and asked to write a book about my life with Bob.

I often think back to that turning point. I had been fortunate in so many ways. First, I'd been able to escape an unjust accusation, but more importantly, I'd been forced to make a change.

Of course, I could never have predicted the precise direction my life was going to take from that point. But there was no doubt that in not getting what I'd wanted, I really had enjoyed the most miraculous good luck.

Wherever You Lay Your Hat

During the making of the movie, Bob and I had to spend a lot of time at Twickenham Film Studios.

It was a very alien environment. The lights, the noise and the unfamiliar faces would have put ninety-nine per cent of cats into a spin, I'm fairly certain. But, despite a little jitteriness at first, Bob adapted quickly.

He would nap when he felt like it. Head off exploring when he wanted.

He worked hard, too. The set designers had created a replica of my flat in north London, where Bob and Luke Treadaway spent their days performing to the cameras. It was long, hard work, but he didn't mind.

The instant Bob heard the tell-tale sound of the bell and saw the recording light in the studio turn from red to green, signalling that filming was over, he would follow the power lines out of the door and up to his dressing room, where he would expect to be fed. There was never a shortage of volunteers. Half the crew carried packets of Dairylea Dunkers or Dreamies with them, ready to cater to Bob's every whim.

Towards the end of filming, someone asked me why he'd adapted so well? It was a good question. My presence was, obviously, important. He felt safe in the knowledge his 'protector' was there. But it was more than that. Bob also liked routine. The predictability and orderliness of his daily existence on the film set made him feel at ease.

But most importantly, I think, Bob had learned that in life you sometimes have to put your head down wherever there's a warm bed. Life is about adapting. About making the most of what's in front of you. And sometimes that means making yourself at home, regardless of where you may lay your hat.

Expect Nothing

One evening, while Bob and I were busking around Covent Garden, we were approached by a very glamorous and attractive young woman. To judge from the way she was dressed – in a glittery black outfit with dazzling jewellery around her neck that must have been worth a small fortune – I think she must have been on her way to the theatre or the opera in the nearby West End.

She saw Bob and me and stopped for a second.

'Oh, how sweet. What a beautiful cat,' she said, smiling, then taking a photograph on her rather expensive-looking phone.

It hadn't been the most profitable evening, so as I often did, I very politely suggested she pop a pound or two into my guitar case for the photo opportunity.

'Any contribution appreciated. It'll go towards a coffee or a treat for Bob here,' I said.

I might as well have asked her if I could pawn the necklace around her neck. Her face was transformed. The smile disappeared to be replaced by a scowl.

'How very impertinent of you,' she said, marching off in a huff.

Such encounters weren't unique. They

simply confirmed something that I'd come to understand even before Bob and I had got together. A truth that unfortunately applies, not only on the streets of London, but everywhere.

Often in life it is best to expect nothing, because that way you will never be disappointed.

Stand Your Ground

The streets of London aren't paved with gold. Quite the opposite. They can be intimidating and unsettling. And Bob had his fair share of scares.

During our days busking and selling *The Big Issue*, he was always particularly aware of dogs. Not necessarily because he was scared of them, but because he knew he had to handle them carefully.

His instincts were so strong that he could tell if a dog was an empty threat. All bark and no bite. A bully, in effect.

It happened very rarely, but in those instances, he would confront them. He would hiss or snarl or even slash his paws at them. It always worked. The dogs themselves either froze, or they fled. I saw Bob reduce several seemingly scary dogs to gibbering jelly.

And whenever he did so, I was reminded that the best way to deal with a bully is to call their bluff.

Judge Others by Actions Not Words

They say that the best way to judge a person's character is by their deeds rather than their words.

With cats, you have no option. You can *only* judge them on their deeds.

Bob has his mischievous moments, of course. And he can be difficult at times. But for more than a decade – through his daily deeds – Bob has displayed exactly the same character. He has been as warm, fun, loyal and caring a companion as anyone could wish to have. No words could convince me that he is otherwise.

Of all the things that Bob has taught me, it is one of the most valuable lessons.

I always try to judge others by the same standards. By their actions and not their words.

Don't Let Your Boat Take in Water

Bob's ability to shut out the rest of the world never ceases to amaze me. He seems to have the capacity to cope with almost any situation.

Perhaps the most unbelievable example of this came in November 2016, when he and I attended the royal premiere of the film of *A Street Cat Named Bob* in London.

It was one of the most surreal evenings of my life, something that, to this day, I can't quite believe happened to me. Bob and I had to appear on the red carpet, doing interviews and posing for photographs. There were dozens, perhaps hundreds of people there, from fans who had travelled to see the event, to television crews and banks of photographers flashing away with their cameras.

It was organised bedlam. At times it was hard to hear above the shouts of the fans, photographers and interviewers who wanted to stick a camera and a microphone in my face. Yet Bob – positioned throughout on my shoulder – sailed through it unfazed.

We spent what must have been half an hour on the red carpet and throughout that time he remained a picture of calm and composure. To be honest, I think he enjoyed it.

That night, everyone asked the same thing: 'How on earth does he do it?'

I can never know for sure, but I think he insulates himself from what is going on around him. I think he simply approaches life with the view that if it isn't directly affecting me, then I have nothing to fear from it.

Boats don't sink because of the water that's around them. Boats sink because of the water that gets into them.

Bob seems to have the gift of not allowing what happens around him to get inside him. He merely sails serenely on.

PART FIVE

The Zen of Bob – How to Be Good to Ourselves

Cats know instinctively how to look after themselves. They don't need to go on fad diets, or hire personal trainers or masseurs to keep themselves fit. They don't need psychologists or life coaches to teach them how to live well.

They just know how to do it – while remaining chilled-out in the process.

That's certainly the case with Bob. Someone once described him as having an inner peace, a 'Zen-like calm' in everything he does. Watching him over the years, I've

seen that we could all learn a little from his
methods, and benefit from what you might
call the Zen of Bob.

Bobfulness

Bob can spend an age staring at a tree full of birds. It's as if he is in a trance. He will sit there, absolutely still, his body coiled, his eyes darting around, picking up every tweet, every flap of a wing. I often wonder what fascinates him so much.

Is it something in his DNA, a hunting instinct? Does he want to get up there and attack them? Is it his fascination with their song? Or is he counting them?

I was watching a programme on TV one day about 'mindfulness' and how it helps the brain to focus on one thing for a few minutes. To think about it, look at it in detail. To get lost in that one small thing, to the exclusion of everything else that's going on around you.

It triggered a thought. That's what Bob is doing when he watches those birds, I smiled to myself.

He's practising Bobfulness.

Rich Cat, Poor Cat

In some ways, Bob's Zen-like calm is a reflection of the simplicity of his life. He has no bills to pay. No mortgage to fret over. No responsibilities.

Bob has no possessions at all. And in that he might be lucky.

It sometimes occurs to me that the more you have, the more you worry about losing it all.

Listen to Your Body

Bob always takes time to stretch. It's as if he's doing yoga or pilates or some other form of exercise. He seems to know instinctively which limbs, which muscles to exercise. It's as if his body has told him what is required.

It never ceases to impress me. And it makes me understand that our bodies are talking to all of us. All the time. Our problem is that most of the time we simply don't listen.

Make a Meal of Your Food

I sometimes watch Bob eating his food. It is fascinating to see. Sometimes he will start off eating eagerly, gobbling down a few mouthfuls. At other times he will inspect it carefully, sniffing and staring at it, as if checking its quality.

When he takes a mouthful, he makes the absolute most of it. He chews away for minutes sometimes, especially if it's a meaty treat that he particularly enjoys. It's as though nothing else matters at that precise moment. As if this is the most important thing in the world. It is a lesson for us.

Doctors, dieticians and wellness experts say that we need to relish and enjoy our food more. There are, apparently, massive benefits to slowing down and relishing every mouthful of food, every sip of a drink. That's because, by paying proper attention to the flavours, smells and textures of what we put in our mouths, even concentrating on the mechanics of eating, it can make us more aware of the sensations that make us feel alive. It can soothe our bodies, lift anxieties and stresses.

Maybe Bob knows this already. Perhaps that is why he puts such importance into eating his food.

S-L-O-W-L-Y Does It

Bob lives his life at his own speed. And that speed is usually pretty leisurely. He can hit the accelerator pedal sometimes. But in general, he will take things s-l-o-w-l-y.

We humans imagine we have too much to do and too little time in which to do it. We never allow ourselves an hour to do something that we can cram into ten or twenty minutes. We somehow think it's wasting time.

But the truth is the absolute opposite. The only thing being wasted is the experience. Especially if you'd benefit from taking an hour to do it. You are actually punishing yourself.

Why would you do that? Why wouldn't you also take things s-l-o-w-l-y?

Know Yourself

The way that Bob manages himself never fails to impress me. He understands himself perfectly, it seems.

He reminds me of one of the wisest pieces of Zen philosophy: 'Knowing others is intelligence; knowing yourself is true wisdom.'

Express How You Feel

Bob wastes no time in letting me know when he's feeling unwell. He makes no pretence about it. He will refuse to move or will lie on my bed, immobile. He will make mewling noises. It's all designed to get the message across: 'I'm not well.'

It is human instinct to deny pain. To soldier on. To deny that we've been hurt or are in discomfort. We leave it until it becomes unbearable.

It's a mistake, of course. Ignore an illness and it is likely to get twice as bad. By acting soon, you give yourself the best chance of recovery.

Tune in to Nature

Cats are tuned into nature in a way that we probably don't yet fully understand. They seem able to detect changes in the weather, and their eating and sleeping habits change considerably through the seasons.

Come the wintertime, for instance, Bob will sleep for hours on end. As the nights close in and the darkness descends, so he curls up and shuts out the outside world. He knows it's the season to hibernate, to recharge the batteries in readiness for spring.

When spring arrives, he sleeps less and is generally more active. Even his body adapts to the change, as he moults and then re-grows his coat according to the seasons.

We might all benefit from paying a little more attention to the natural cycle of things.

Say What You Mean, and Mean What You Say

Bob communicates using a mixture of sounds – from gentle purrs and growls, to hisses and blood-curdling screams. But he can also get his message across using body language, swishing and wagging his tail, or arching his body to make a particular point. What's most impressive about it all is its simplicity. If he's got something to say, he gets it across quickly and directly. There is never any room for doubt.

First thing in the morning, he will slide up along the bed and alert me to the fact that it's his breakfast time. He may use a variety of methods for this: from purring quietly to jumping forcefully on to my chest, or placing his face inches from mine and letting out an ear-piercing *meow*.

Whatever method he uses, however, his message is unmistakeable. I open my eyes and there he is, staring at me with an expression that says: 'Come on, get up, I'm hungry.'

I don't always appreciate it, especially if he wakes me at the crack of dawn on a cold, winter's morning. But in a world where we can all sometimes take a hundred words when one will do, I have come to admire his directness.

Bob doesn't do small talk. It's all big talk. He says what he means – and means what he says.

No Means No

With Bob, no means precisely that. No.

If he doesn't want to do something, then that's that. He won't do it. No treat, no enticement, no stroke of the head or back will move him. He has made up his mind. End of story. I might as well give up.

It actually makes life simpler. It keeps things black and white. There are no shades of grey. You accept his decision, and move on. You find an alternative route, or a different way of doing things. No matter how inconvenient or annoying it may be.

Sometimes, as adults, we all need to learn to say no. It's our right to do so. Clearly and simply and unambiguously. It may not make everyone happy, all the time. But at least people will know where you – and they – stand.

A Simple Thank You

Bob's tail is a signalling system all of its own.

If he is swishing it sharply from side to side, it means he is agitated or upset. But if it is moving more slowly and rhythmically – like a windscreen wiper – it's a sign of contentment. All is well in his world.

I've often wondered why he feels the need to signal this way. I'm sure it isn't for my benefit. Regardless, I always appreciate seeing that tell-tale, slow-motion wag. To me, it's as good as him writing me a thank-you note, or sending flowers or a box of chocolates.

If only others did the same, even unconsciously.

Silence Is Golden

Bob has a language all of his own – a highly effective system for communicating precisely what he wants to say. I find it fascinating to behold. It has taught me a lot of useful things about the art of communication.

There are days, for example, when Bob will sit alongside me barely making a sound from dawn 'til dusk. I never worry about it. It must mean that he is content. If he wasn't, he would let me know soon enough.

I often nod and smile wistfully at him. If only that were true in the human world, I think to myself. So many people speak when they have nothing to say. When they would also be better off appreciating that sometimes silence really is golden.

That the quieter you become, the more you can hear.

A Social Network

When Bob and I did our first book signings, I received a number of surprises. For a start, I was amazed – and genuinely moved – by the number of people who turned up to meet us. It was something of a miracle, as far as I was concerned. I didn't think anyone would be interested.

But the other really surprising thing was the way Bob reacted to all this attention. He seemed genuinely to lap it up. He didn't mind people stroking him, within reason. He remained completely in control. If he felt like napping, that's exactly what he did. And if it was time to go home, then he let me know that in no uncertain terms. But in the main he was happy to interact with people, especially those that had treats for him.

It set me thinking. There are lots of scientific studies that argue human health and wellbeing is improved by regular, social interaction. In short, isolation is bad for you, but mixing with people – even if it's for a chat in a shop or the park – is good for you.

I suspect, again, that cats know this. It's one of the reasons they have gravitated towards us humans.

Let the Love In

I'm sure everyone who has ever had or known a cat will agree with me on this universal truth: they never, ever refuse affection. Bob certainly doesn't. Start tickling him under his neck, or stroking the back of his neck, and he will press his head against you and lie there. It's as if he's saying: 'Yes, I deserve this attention, please continue.'

Sometimes, if he feels the need, he will flip himself over and spread himself out, inviting you to direct your tickling to his tummy instead. He absolutely loves it and can't get enough of it. I've never spent more than a few minutes stroking him, but I reckon if I carried on for an hour, he'd be perfectly happy.

It occurred to me once that we could all learn from this. Too many of us reject genuine and sincere affection, whether it is from a friend or a relative, or someone we love. I know I've been guilty of this. We do so for many reasons: fear, embarrassment, self-doubt.

It makes no sense when you think about it. Love is in short supply in this world, so when it is offered to us, we should all embrace it. We should all follow Bob's lead. We should all let the love in.

Have Fun – and Often

Bob is no different to other cats when it comes to play. He loves nothing more than to flip a favourite toy around the room, or to leap manically up and down trying to catch the sunbeams that are dancing on the wall. At Christmas, he can entertain himself for ages with a piece of used wrapping paper.

It's as though he is lost in his own world, motivated by who knows what. Is he trying to catch the mouse, or simply exhilarated by the fun of tossing it around the room? Is he intent on tearing the Christmas wrapping into pieces, or does he just love the sound and sensation of the crumpled paper? Who knows. And more importantly, who cares?

What's clear is that it provides him with entertainment, a break from his normal routine. And when he's doing it, the rest of the world is shut out completely. We all need to do that every now and again, don't we?

Don't Be Slaves to the Clock

Bob, like all cats, obeys his body clock. He knows when the day begins, and when it ends. When it's time to sleep and eat. *Especially,* when it's time to eat. But beyond that, time – as we know it – is of little importance to him. There is no clock dictating how he whiles away the hours each day.

We are very different, of course. We are slaves to the clock. We dwell on the passing of time, mourn the way moments flash by. We are constantly counting the hours, days, months and years.

We could learn a lot from Bob's attitude. We might live more enjoyable, more fulfilling lives. Maybe even longer ones, too?

Pay No Heed to What Others Think of You

Cats aren't burdened by worrying about what other cats think of them. Well, as far as we know, at least.

I'm pretty convinced that Bob isn't obsessed with his reputation. He's not concerned about how many people 'like' him on social media. (Even though many thousands do.) He isn't at all concerned with what people say about him publicly. He's oblivious to it. Bob just gets on with being himself. Living his day-to-day life and, in doing so, displaying his true character. If that appeals to people, then great. If it doesn't, no matter. He is who he is — and that's the way it is.

If only we could all adopt that attitude.

Too many of us are eaten up by worrying about what others think and say about us. We would be better off focusing on our true character rather than 'reputations' that can rise and fall for no good reason. Being ourselves, saying what we really feel.

That, after all, is the truth. And that's what counts in the end.

Live the Years, Don't Count Them

As I write, Bob is now around eleven years old. Perhaps older. As a housebound cat, there's every possibility he will live well into his teens, even into his twenties. He has no awareness of this, of course. He may be in his middle years now, but he is not going to have a mid-life crisis.

He isn't going to suddenly do something dramatic like buy a sports car or run off to a Buddhist retreat in Nepal. He's not going to totally re-invent himself because he is suddenly aware of his mortality.

We can never know this, but I imagine that ageing is simply something he feels. He is not counting the years. He is simply living them. Wouldn't we all benefit from thinking that way sometimes? None of us has to be defined by our chronological age.

Age really is just a number.

Don't Grow Up

Bob may be older, but he is definitely still in touch with his inner kitten. The younger, more playful part of him is always there.

Sometimes he will play with a toy, chase the reflection of glass on the wall. At other times he will find a cardboard box or a piece of paper and entertain himself by playing with it.

It's proof of something that I heard once: it is easier to grow old if you haven't entirely grown up. Perhaps we should all see the world that way.

It's the Life in Your Years

Even as he gets older, Bob lives his life to the full, doing precisely what he wants, when he wants to do it.

If he wants to spend his day curled up in a ball watching the world go by, he will do so. If he wants to spend it playing or chasing things around the house, he will do so. He is living on his own terms, oblivious to the passing of time.

Sometimes I look at him and think he is an embodiment of another old saying: 'It's not the years in your life that count, it's the life in your years.'

Stay Open to Change

As Bob has grown older, he has subtly changed his ways.

He gives himself more time to rest and recuperate. If he's had a busy day, he will sleep an extra hour. He may also start his day a little later the following morning. And he will not be rushed in that process. His eating habits have changed slightly, too. He prefers to eat soft food in the evening now – and likes to eat at 7.30 p.m. Precisely.

It has all happened naturally and seamlessly. It's as if his body is telling him that it needs to modify itself. It is something we could all learn from. We all need to stay open to change.

PART SIX

The University of Bob – Lessons in Day-to-Day Life

Sharing my life with Bob is an endless education. There's something new to be learned every day. Sometimes it is simply from watching him interacting with the world around him. At other times it's the situations that we find ourselves in – both at home and on our travels together.

It's as if I've enrolled as a lifetime student at the University of Bob.

Fall Down Seven Times, Get Up Eight

I'd arranged to get together with an old friend, Steve, for a drink one summer's evening.

We were in the middle of a heatwave, so we sat out in the beer garden. I hung my rucksack on a hook that was attached to the wall, about five feet off the ground. Bob sat on the bench beside me, lapping up the last rays of sunshine.

I left him and Steve while I popped inside to the bar. When I came back, Steve was smiling broadly.

'What's so funny?' I asked.

'Bob's been entertaining me,' he said.

'What's he been up to?'

'He's been trying to snatch something from your bag. I wasn't sure whether to let him have it or not,' he replied, pointing at the rucksack, and the distinctive colouring of a packet of snacks that was sticking out from one of the pockets.

'Ah, they're his favourite treats. So, what did he do?'

'It's been hilarious. First, he tried jumping straight up in the air to snatch it. But that didn't work. So then he tried balancing on that chair there, but it wouldn't hold his weight.'

I was laughing myself now.

'He came close once,' Steve said. 'He jumped off the table and managed to grab a hold of the side of the bag. He was hanging on for grim life with his claws. But he couldn't hold it and slipped back down again, like a cartoon character.'

I gave Bob a ruffle on the back of his neck.

'You never give up, do you, mate,' I said.

I then reached for the snacks from the rucksack and gave him a couple of treats.

Steve couldn't help smiling. He was something of a philosopher. Or liked to think he was, at least.

'They say that's the secret of life,' he said.

'What is?'

'Fall down seven times, get up eight.'

I smiled. He was right. We should never give in. Perseverance always pays off.

Trust Your Instincts

Bob and I were walking through the West End, on our way home after a meeting. I'd decided to head in the direction of our old 'pitch' on Neal Street, where my old friend Sam co-ordinated sales of *The Big Issue* to the area's small army of vendors. I hadn't seen her for a while and wanted to say hello.

We'd not been walking for long when Bob started getting agitated, turning around in circles on my shoulder and making a loud mewling sound.

I placed him down on the pavement and gave him a snack, then pressed on. He was still unhappy. I'd walked a couple of hundred yards down another street, when I saw a commotion on the corner ahead of me.

Black smoke was billowing into the air and I could hear fire-engine sirens drawing closer. There were already men in yellow coats cordoning off the area and tourists and shoppers were being hurriedly shepherded away from the scene.

It was obvious there was a major incident, a fire or perhaps worse, some kind of terrorist incident. So I put Bob on my shoulders and took a circuitous route back to the railway station, from where we would head home to Surrey.

Thankfully, I learned later from Sam that the incident was a small, household fire, caused by someone leaving their kitchen hob on. No one had been hurt. But it could easily have been something much worse. The incident stuck in my mind, because of the way Bob reacted.

Cats have highly developed senses that allow them to detect things that we humans cannot, such as earthquakes and major storms. They can also pick up on human illness, epilepsy in particular. Bob had intuitively picked up on something in the West End. Fortunately, my instinct had been to listen to him.

It reinforced something that I had long believed in. That we should all listen to our instincts, to our gut feelings. They are invariably right.

Change One Person's World

Bob and I were sitting in a doorway, taking shelter from the rain. It was literally bouncing off the pavement; there was little prospect of us selling any magazines.

But then, out of nowhere, we were approached by a very striking young lady. She was pretty with dark hair and was wearing a yellow raincoat.

Judging from her accent, she was Russian – or something like that. She leaned down and gave Bob a gentle ruffle on the back of the neck. I noticed that she was wearing a bracelet with an inscription in another language. I asked her what it meant.

She smiled. 'It's an expression from Estonia. Where I'm from. It says: Who does not thank for little, will not thank for much.'

'How true that is,' I said, smiling back.

She spent a few minutes with us, chatting quietly about nothing in particular. She gave me a couple of pounds for a magazine, before giving Bob a final nuzzle and heading off.

'Thank you,' she said.

I gave her a little hug.

'No, thank you,' I said.

The biggest impact can sometimes come from the smallest acts. What that lady did that evening was such a little thing. It took her only a few moments, but it meant a great deal to me. You don't have to change the whole world to help someone, sometimes it's enough to change that person's world for a few moments.

Find Your Bliss

When Bob and I were busking, I was always surprised at how relaxed he was, sitting amongst the crowds in Covent Garden and around Piccadilly.

On the rare occasion he did get agitated, there was something that was always liable to calm him down: music. As soon as I started strumming away at my guitar, his body language changed. He seemed more mellow. His tail-wagging fell into the distinctive, wind-screen-wiper pattern that indicated he was happy. That he had found his own form of bliss.

More recently, if I am recording music in my little studio at home, he has to sit directly behind me when the sound is booming out. No matter how loud it gets, and it can get very loud, he wants to be there.

Music has, at various times, been my own salvation. Seeing its impact on Bob has underlined to me that we all have something that has the power to soothe, restore and lift us when we need it.

We all need to find our bliss sometimes.

The Courage to Ask

I was sitting outside a coffee shop in Islington with Bob. It was a very hippyish place; inside the walls were covered in little bits of philosophy. Sayings, mantras. Little slices of wisdom.

One had jumped out at me as I'd ordered my coffee.

'Be strong enough to stand alone, smart enough to know when you need help and brave enough to ask for it.'

It made me think immediately of Bob.

When he'd been injured, he had managed to remove himself from the danger he faced and position himself in my block of flats. He had somehow worked out that it was his best chance of getting some help. As it turned out, his instincts had brought him to me.

Of course, his experience echoed my own. When I'd been homeless, I'd put myself in terrible danger. But I'd found the strength to remove myself, to recognise that I needed to beat my drug addiction and to seek out the treatment I needed.

These days, when I'm doing charity work, I am frequently asked to offer advice to addicts or homeless people who feel lost and unable to escape their fates. I often refer to that saying in the coffee shop.

At our lowest ebbs, we all need to find the strength to stand alone, the intelligence to know we need help – and, most of all, the courage to ask.

New Isn't Always Better

Bob's favourite toy for many years was his 'raggedy' mouse. It was a battered old fabric animal with buttons for eyes and a string tail. He loved tugging and tearing at it, flinging and flipping it around the room so that he could chase after it. After a while it became a tattered rag, a shapeless shadow of its former self, but he didn't care. Bob loved the thing. He could while away hours playing with it.

I tried replacing it a couple of times, swapping it for newer toys, but he didn't take an interest in any of them. Instead he stalked the flat looking for his old mouse. Once I put it in the bin, but even then he sniffed it out.

I was genuinely worried that it might be harmful to him, that the old fabric might be infected. And I was sure that he should have something newer, shinier, more exciting. But I was totally missing the point.

I was seeing things from my perspective. To me his raggedy mouse was a sad, broken thing. Fit only for the dustbin. But Bob saw it completely differently. It was his toy. It made him happy. It provided him with stimulation, entertainment and escape. He didn't need anything else. He kept it for years after that.

Everyone today is so obsessed with having the new version of everything. The latest version phone, laptop, video game, fashion item. But why? If they are doing their job, do we really need them? Is new necessarily better? If we stopped and thought about it, we'd probably be just as happy with what we already have.

Silver Linings

Working with Bob on the set of the movie about us was demanding work – and not only because we often had to get up at 5 a.m. in the morning to get to the set on time.

Unlike the 'professional' cats on the set, Bob wasn't trained to act for the cameras and would frequently do unpredictable things. Often, for instance, he would drop his head or turn around, when the cameramen wanted him to look directly into the lens.

I had to develop a repertoire of tricks and ploys to keep his eye-line where the cameraman needed it to be. I did everything from positioning myself behind the camera, clicking my fingers, to pointing a laser pen at the walls to make him look around the room.

It was inevitable that he wouldn't always stick to the script. But the director, Roger Spottiswoode, used Bob's odd moments of improvisation to good effect.

One day, rather than sitting still for the camera as required, Bob started chasing the laser pen around the room. Roger kept the cameras going and used the footage in another scene in which Bob is seen pursuing a mouse.

It was a reminder that life rarely goes exactly to plan. But we can always turn difficulties to our advantage. Every cloud has a silver lining, as they say. We should always look for that positive.

We All Have Something to Give

It was a week before Christmas and Bob and I were struggling to make ends meet during a spell of cold weather. We were busking near Shaftesbury Avenue one evening, when a Salvation Army band and choir arrived and began singing the Christmas carol, 'In the Bleak Midwinter.' I found myself drawn in by the words, in particular to the final verse:

What can I give Him, poor as I am?

If I were a shepherd, I would bring a
lamb.

If I were a Wise Man, I would do my
part;

Yet what I can I give Him: give my heart.

Times were hard and I suddenly felt sorry for myself.

Ha, I thought. What do I have to give? Nothing.

But I was wrong.

Just then a lady passed by. She was in her fifties, smartly dressed, but looking a little emotional.

'Would you mind if I had a moment with him?' she said, seeing Bob. 'Of course,' I replied.

As she sat and stroked Bob, we began chatting. It turned out it was the anniversary of her son's death. She was no longer married to the boy's father and was heading home to an empty house. She'd had a cat, but it had died six months earlier, too.

'I'm dreading tonight,' she said, dabbing away a tear. 'I'll be all alone there with my memories. You are so lucky to have Bob here with you.'

It stopped me in my tracks. I felt such a fool.

We all have something to give. No matter how small or trivial we might think it is, it could mean the world to someone else. No matter how sorry we are feeling for ourselves, we should never forget it.

The Power of Hope

Bob seems to be able to lift and inspire people wherever we go. He has put smiles on faces, young and old. Moved many to tears. To be honest, it was hard for me to understand this at first. How could the story of a cat helping to transform the life of a troubled young man have touched so many people in so many parts of the world?

An encounter in Oslo, in Norway, shone a light.

Our publishers there had arranged for Bob to meet a lady called Anne. She was blind, but had read the Braille versions of our books and become one of our biggest fans in Norway.

She was beside herself with joy at meeting Bob, even though – obviously – she couldn't see him.

He doesn't always respond to being touched, especially in busy situations, but when she began stroking him, he reciprocated by rubbing his head against her. It was as if he sensed how important this moment was to her.

Through an interpreter, someone asked her what it was that had struck such a powerful chord in her. Her answer came down to one word: hope.

The hope she'd seen in the story of Bob and me had shone light in her darkness, she said. It had given her hope where, often, she'd not had very much at all. It was a simple answer. And a profound one, too. It made me realise that we all need to feel hope. And it doesn't matter where we see or find it.

We Are Not Alone

In 2017, Bob and I were fortunate enough to visit Tokyo to attend the Japanese premiere of the movie of *A Street Cat Named Bob*.

Away from all the glamour, the most affecting moment came when we were introduced to two *The Big Issue* sellers, Akira and

Shinzo. Shinzo had a cat, too, a stray that he had named Mi. He had been living a pretty simple existence, living off scraps of food and sleeping rough. He'd tried selling *The Big Issue*, but found it very hard going. He couldn't attract people's attention. Mi had changed his fortunes immediately.

'People were more open to me,' he said. 'They stopped and talked.'

Akira had a similar story. He had briefly found a cat abandoned in a park. He had looked after it for two weeks before it was reunited with its owner. In that fortnight, he'd started taking the cat with him to sell *The Big Issue* outside the main railway station, where he had his pitch.

'I was no longer invisible. You know how that feels?' he said to me.

'Yes, I do,' I nodded. I told him that it had only been when Bob had come into my life that people had 'seen' me.

It was as if I was looking into a mirror. We all think we are unique. That no one can have had it is as bad as us. That is wrong.

No matter how desperate your situation. No matter how isolated and alone you might feel, the truth is you aren't alone at all. There is someone out there just like you. Going through the same things. It needed Bob to take me to the other side of the world to show me that.

Never Waste a Second Chance

Bob and I were far from home, at a book signing in Berlin.

We'd been busy meeting people for about an hour, when I looked up into the long queue and was drawn to a face in the crowd. At first, I couldn't quite believe it. It can't be her, I told myself. What was she doing here in Germany? But as she drew closer and closer to the front of the line, I saw that it really was her. I don't want to identify her, so let's call her Hannah.

Around eight or nine years ago, Hannah's life had been as much of a mess as mine. She, too, had been homeless and addicted to heroin. We had often slept rough in the same places in London. I hadn't seen her since those dark days.

Now, to my utter amazement, here she was — standing in line in a bookshop in Berlin. We met up afterwards and caught up. She told me that she had left London and her past to make a new life for herself. She told me that she was clean and in a relationship. Her face positively glowed with health and happiness. We promised each other that we would see each other again. (And we did. I returned to Berlin afterwards to spend more time with her.)

It was only in the days and hours that followed, the significance of the moment hit home. Like Hannah, I know that the battle against addiction is a daily one. It doesn't go away. It never will. But we have both found hope. And we can see the way ahead. Many of those with whom we shared those dark and distant days on the street were not so fortunate. We were the lucky ones that got out alive.

We are all gifted second chances in life. But those chances are worthless, unless we learn from the mistakes we made first time around.

There But For the Grace of God . . .

We were walking through the West End one winter evening, when Bob started getting agitated. At first, I thought it was the cold weather, but then I realised we were being followed.

Like Bob, I'd developed a radar for this over the years. I turned and spotted the guy in the throng. He was a young, slightly built lad, with greasy hair and a rucksack on his back.

We needed to cut through a small alleyway to get to the station. We'd barely entered the narrow street, when Bob let out a loud, *whew* noise. The young guy had lurched at us, grabbing at my rucksack.

I'm quite capable of looking after myself – as is Bob. Between us we pushed him away. He ran off, but only made it a few yards before he tripped and fell to the ground. The kid hauled himself to his knees and started crying.

Rather than send him off, I sat with him for a few minutes, talking. I could see he was desperate. He'd run away from an abusive home in the north of England without a penny to his name. He hadn't had a decent night's sleep in a week and had barely eaten. I told him about the best shelters to go to and wrote down a couple of phone numbers for charities that I knew might help. I also gave him some money. It was the least I could do.

If there was one lesson I'd learned during my time sleeping rough, it was that life on the streets dehumanises people. The desperation, loneliness and lack of decent, human contact drags you down. And in the process, you lose all sense of yourself – of what's right and wrong. It had happened to me.

In fact, I could see my younger self in this lad.

We are all too quick to rush to judgment. We all forget that, with a tiny twist of fate, any one of us could find ourselves on the street.

There, but for the grace of God, go all of us.

Don't Forget Where You Came From

Bob and I were approaching the end of a big book signing in London. We'd been meeting and greeting people for three hours and there was still a huge queue snaking around the store.

The managers of the bookshop had decided that they couldn't let any more people in. Reluctantly, I'd agreed to let them stop anyone else joining the line.

As usual, I had a couple of trusty friends helping me. One of them came in looking concerned. 'There's a mother and daughter here who caught the train down this morning from Glasgow. The train got delayed and they've just got here. They've been told they can't meet you and Bob. They're really upset.'

'Tell them to hang around,' I whispered in his ear.

At the end of the signing, the friend led them over. I let them sit down and stroke Bob for a minute while we chatted. I'd expected him to be exhausted by the end of a marathon signing, but he was as good as gold with them.

'We're so grateful,' the daughter said as, eventually, I told them we'd have to head off. 'It's Mum's birthday.'

I smiled.

'I think you've got it wrong there,' I said, giving the mother a hug. 'It's me who should be grateful. Without people like you, I'd never have made it off the streets.'

We're all guilty of forgetting our origins sometimes. But we shouldn't ever forget how we got to where we are in our lives

– and to be thankful to those who helped us get there.

Let Life Surprise You

To say that the recent transformation in my life was a surprise would be the understatement of the century. Never in a million years would I have imagined I'd be approached to write a book about my friendship with Bob. Never in a million years would I have anticipated that it would become a bestseller around the world.

And if I had told anyone that it would be turned into a movie, and premiered in the West End with Bob and I being introduced to the future Queen of England beforehand, then quite rightly, they would have thought I was utterly insane. Yet it did happen.

It's been said that wisdom is the ability to learn from change. Well, if I haven't acquired some wisdom – some perspective – from the massive changes that have occurred in my life, there is little hope for me. One of the simplest things I've learned is that sometimes you have to let fate play its hand.

Sometimes the best things happen unexpectedly. For seemingly no reason at all. There's nothing you can do about it. So the best thing you can do is just let go.

Let go – and let life surprise you.

Money Can't Buy You Love

Bob and I were sitting in a very swanky hotel room in Tokyo. It had been a busy day and I'd treated us to a really nice dinner, on room service: a delicious steak for me and gourmet chicken cat food for Bob. It truly was five-star luxury.

As I sat there enjoying my meal, I couldn't help but think back over our time together and other, much less fancy meals we'd had. I remembered the first night that we'd gone busking together in Covent Garden and how, thanks to Bob's charisma, I'd earned two or three times what I would normally have earned. I'd treated myself to a curry and him to a tin of tuna. Back then I'd been used to eating from tins. Or living simply off breakfast cereal.

So what was different tonight? The truth was, nothing really. Yes, the food was being served on fine china and the wine was a very good vintage. But certainly as far as Bob was concerned, it didn't matter.

To Bob it was of absolutely no significance whether we were in a five-star hotel or a fifth-floor flat. It didn't matter whether I had fifty pence or fifty pounds in my pocket.

Money, wealth, whatever you want to call it, is a transient thing. It comes and it goes. We all go through periods of feast and famine. Times when we feel – financially, at least – rich and poor. But that is only ever part of the picture.

Money doesn't give us the most important things of all in life. It certainly doesn't buy us love.

As we ate like kings in our Tokyo suite, I gave Bob a little ruffle. Even if I was to end up back on the street, I would still be a rich man.

As long as I had him with me.

Acknowledgements

I coudn't possibly let a book like this end without drawing on another piece of wisdom that I've picked up during my time with Bob: the importance of saying thank you. It's been six years now since my first, tentative steps into the world of publishing. Back in 2012, when *A Street Cat Named Bob* was first published, I was more than a little daunted by it all. But now – half a dozen books later – each new project seems like a reunion with old and trusted friends. That's certainly the case with Rowena Webb, my publisher at Hodder and Stoughton, who first took me on all those years ago and whose idea has now provided the spark for this book. She therefore must get my first thanks. I'd also like to single out Kerry Hood, Rosie Stephen, Ian Wong and the rest of the talented team at Hodder, as well as Dan Williams for his adorable illustrations. Thanks must also go to my agent Lesley Thorne and everyone at Aitken Alexander for all the work they do on my behalf. I really appreciate it. Last – but definitely not least – I must again thank Garry Jenkins, who has been on this journey the longest of all, since Bob and I first met him on a wintry day outside the Angel, Islington in December 2010, in fact. Somehow, he always manages to find the right words – although, I suspect, even he probably doesn't have enough of them to sum up the debt of gratitude I owe him. So I'll end where I began, by just saying thank you.

THE LITTLE BOOK OF BOB

To find out more about James
and Bob, visit their website at

www.streetcatbob.world

You can also follow them on Twitter
at www.twitter.com/streetcatbob,
or visit their Facebook page at
www.facebook.com/streetcatbob for
the latest news, stories and pictures.